Spoken Tokens

A Short Book of Vocal Verse

Becky Askin

Print information available on the last page

Rev. date: 05/22/2019

To order additional copies of this book, contact:
Xlibris
1-888-795-4274
www.Xlibris.com
Orders@Xlibris.com

Spoken Tokens
by
Becky Askin

Dedicated to
Askin/Benzinger
offspring/ancestors

Winter a Mile in on a Dirt Road

Bitter cold and windy too, the winter weather's here.
Minus ten the meter reads, the air is crisp and clear.
Frozen crystals on the glass refract the morning light.
Pinks and purples bring the sun: a wondrous winter sight.

Lying 'neath the comforter, feeling snug and warm.
Hear the husband close the door, he steps into the storm.
Hear him try to start the truck, engine's really whirring;
Must get up and start to dress, consciousness is stirring.

Breakfast done and lunch is made, my turn now to go.
Push against the frozen door, step into the snow.
Crunchy sounds beneath my feet; snow blown on the deck;
Rosy cheeks and tear-filled eyes, wind blows down my neck.

Icy layers on the windows, starting up the car,
On the way to work at last, seems so very far.

PIANOS

An old upright in Snyder, with a brassy sound;
Rhapsody in Blue was victim to my fingers' pound.

"Butterfly" was played on stage at 6th grade graduation,
Starting years of jealousy but also acclamation.

Beethoven's Fifth Symphony, arranged as a duet—
Somewhere's a recording of that on an old cassette.

New York's Regents judged my playing year by year by year;
A Chopin nocturne earned their medals and some cheer.

College days: Prokofiev's Third Concerto was the major thing;
Practice rooms and concert halls made my fingers sing.

Played on many keyboards both in Europe and at home;
"Solfizietto's" notes rang out wherever I would roam.

In Salzburg's Mozarteum or Santa Barbara's baggage claim;
I would sit and play a waltz while others played a cribbage game.

All my students' pianos too have felt my fingers' pressing.
Some were grand and excellent, others quite depressing.

But the keyboards I'll remember are the ones at which I wrote
The many songs and pieces I've composed and played by rote.

(*There actually is an old piano up against the wall in the Santa Barbara airport baggage claim room for people to play who are waiting for their bags.)

She-We-He-Me

I keep encountering me,
In we and he and she.
Those three there plus me
So often disagree.

And nothing is for certain.
There is no guarantee.
We live behind a curtain,
And think that we can see.

The Sleeper

The whirring of the metal wheels rolling on the track;
Little bumps of train track sections cause the click and clack.
Snug inside a tiny sleeper, lulled by motion, darkness, sound;
Shielded from external issues, consciousness is dream-state bound.
No one knows you, you know no one, time itself suspended.
Destination's straight ahead but normal life's upended.
Where we are in space and time is relative to what?
Knowing is perception but there always is a 'but.'

PAPER MAPS

Going on a trip, and need to find the way.
Jet Pak and iPad, Samsung phone and hey!
Maggie and Gertie.* Don't forget the map.
Five devices get us there so I can take a nap.

*GPS trackers

TRAIN WAVERS

No less than five, the number of people
Who stand by the track and wave to the train.
The windows are darkened, they can't see my wave-back,
So that means they wave without gain.
Where else can you find, in all of mankind:
The wish to send cheer without fear?
For gone is the train, the wave's in the past,
It all happened in less than an hour.
The greeting, the wave and the smile were sent out,
Passed forward, the residual power.

Sleeping Digs

a patio in Snyder, a B & B in Utah
a pension in France and a youth hostel in Austria
a castle south of Germany, a cruise ship in the Caribbean
simple cabins by Twin Lakes, a long train into Mexico
a bus trip to New Jersey, a truck bed in New York
my Volvo up at Lassen Park, a camper by the redwoods
a ferry on the way to Greece, Plymouth wagon: Canada
a prop plane all the way to London, condo in Kauai
apartment by the Golden Gate, punch-bug: Adirondacks
stand-up tent: Yosemite, rented house in Concord
castles, campers, ferries, boats: slept on many things that float
shelters for a body resting, different sites for human nesting

<u>BEING</u>

Longing, yearning, learning, stumbling –
On a path to where?
Proving, striving, trying, fumbling –
Wanting to be there.
Craving, seeking, speaking, grumbling –
Climbing rocky trails.
Knocking, growing, sowing, tumbling –
Tossed in earthly gales.
Moving, clearing, hearing, mumbling –
Boulders in your way.
Praying, stilling, willing, rumbling –
Obstacles you slay.
Aiding, caring, sharing, crumbling –
You will get to there.
Working, searching, serving, humbling –
Just: you don't know where.

BEETHOVEN'S MUSIC

Noisy directness and terrible fury:
Where are we going in such a great hurry?
Unbuttoned wrath, and unrelenting toughness.
Who thought that music could have such boisterous roughness?

♪

Irritable piquancy and humorous intensity:
Expectations of a truly grandiose propensity.
Concentrated savagery and overflowing tension
Fill us with objections and a certain apprehension.

♪

Then we're shot with mystery or serious conjecture:
Overflowing measures of a complicated texture.
Nature in its wildness, with strains of lofty elegance
Can't erase the fearfulness of the embodied violence.

♪

Strains of good humor, spontaneous pluck;
Tells us he thought there was no thing as luck.
Rather like life there's intense repetition;
Melodies sing of the human condition.

WHO CARES

Who cares all the places he's been.
Who cares about his views of sin.
Who cares what he thinks or he feels.
Who cares if he's hurt or he heals.
Who cares if he breathes or he doesn't.
Who cares if he will or he won't.
Who cares what if, what or when.
Who cares: no one. And so,
Say, "Amen."

PERFORMANCE

The performance just happens; the glitter and the lights;
Solo playing: quite unnerving: she is quite the star.
Everyone will judge her; she has reached great heights
Her uniquely artsy gift becomes now the new par.
Jealousy just happens; people must survive.
The desire for approval authors every drive.

Does she go forth and succeed? Does she bend to the resentment?
Does she let her talent shine? What is there of true contentment?

Underneath a brimming bushel, put there by submission;
Lies the talent of a person, a superb musician.
Female born, a careful one, she's learned to let it go.
Education taught her well: she'll try not to out-glow.
Thus the world turns: halting ego, forever unsure.
Joy in life has been replaced; now she must endure.

💧CONDENSATION💧

Silently the frozen moisture on my window changes,
Droplets merge and fall, the warmed liquid rearranges.
The spotted pane is now all lined with tracks and running rivers.
Into a tiny pool on the window's sill, a track delivers.

And now another pool is forming elsewhere on the sill,
It wanders to the edge with its own seeming focused will.
A few more drops cause it to overflow and neatly drop,
A puddle on the floor is each small drop's last stop.

HANDS OF SERVICE

A child of three softly looks at her hands,
gazing around at her world so immense;
Learning of life through each physical sense,
closing her soul-life to worldly demands.

A teenager catches a glimpse of her hands,
pausing amid ego-testing and trial;
Caught between ardent embrace or denial,
oblivious to the assault of her glands.

A middle aged woman remarks at her hands;
once so pretty and smooth in the beauty of youth;
Now reflecting her life, not concealing its truth:
each spot, mole or wrinkle a story commands.

A woman of sixty stares down at her hands,
pondering life from before and again;
Daring to face the unquestioned amen,
counting the dwindling hourglass sands.

If they have sown service, this woman's two hands,
if they have been used for the pure and the good,
If they have done always the best that they could,
they reach forth in faith when the death call demands.

BEING HERE AND NOW

H e r e a n d n o w :
B e I n g

T h e r e a n d t h e n :
S e e I n g

L i f e ' s t h e s a m e f o r a l l o f u s

K n o w I n g t h I s :

F r e e I n g

THE GAME OF LIFE

You might as well just relax and enjoy:
The whole thing's out of your hands.
The game of life is like a toy:
It depends where your man lands.

You spin the dial but the dial's fixed:
You'll land on A, B or C.
You shuffle the cards, get the deck all mixed,
But whatever you're dealt will be.

You can play it safe, you can play it hard.
You can struggle to win and cheat.
You can sweat it out over every card,
You can challenge all you meet.

Or you can simply realize
That win or lose you'll be
Much happier if in all your tries
You let be what will be.

So you might as well just relax and enjoy
And give that dial a happy spin.
The game of life is just like a toy,
Sometimes you lose and sometimes you win.

An infrequent sentiment that causes one to mumble:
Touching an immensity that oft makes one feel humble.
Energized with pleasure seeing something odd or rare.
Brain activity is stretching, trying to compare.

Unexpected beauty, man's uncommon feats,
Commonplace routine, the novelty unseats.
Ordinary models, patterns versions or ideals
Cannot bring the goose bumps that the skin now feels.

New perspectives cause the mind and body to engage;
Something new has split the old and plopped itself onstage.
On the frontier one may feel fear, inference is spurious;
All because we humans cannot help our being curious.

ALONE

No one has patience
With her tears
No one has time
To hear her fears
dealing with their own woes … that is simply how it goes
No one knows meaning
As her end nears

ON THE DEATH OF ERIC'S FATHER

Your father, my father - what is the difference?

A parent who cared - as best as they could
Will be missed by us all - as rightly they should

Our being flows forward - one day at a time
But the reminder of death - tolls
a deep special chime

Our purpose is questioned - our life path is jiggled
The unknown awaits us - security's wiggled

We're grateful for lots - still afraid of the rest
Many questions unanswered - are
we cursed or still blessed

Your father has died - and I feel now your pain
Which brings us together - on this physical plane

Your father my father - there is no difference.

PERCEPTION

Observation, recognition, we try out a meaning.
Light and shadow, color nuance, which way is it leaning?
Senses feed us, thought takes over: sorting, ranking, forming.
Happens automatically: business of transforming.

Time Change

Set the clocks - ahead,behind.
Now reset the body's mind.
Everything is relative,
Despite the newer perspective.
Modify the habit blueprint,
Break with the routine.
Change the custom, flout the practice,
Make a brand new scene.

Ode to Hippiedom - 1970

It's on the streets of SF where she stands in hippie gear;
Trusting inexperience to mitigate the fear.
Trying to reach America and force her to resign;
Playing her harmonica and flashing the peace sign.

Long dress and no underwear. Why bother? Cramps the style.
Macrame'ing purses: such a trek into denial.
Looking up to see it's noon, the silver bracelets jingle;
With her kindred brothers and her sisters she will mingle.

Slipping off her Birkenstocks, she sits to meditate.
Trying to still the mind and body; simply vegetate.
Then a reading from *The Prophet* or the famed *I Ching*.
Making one with the great Oneness through an endless reaching.

Millet casserole for dinner, goat milk birthday cake.
Hands are red from first-time gard'ning, burned from brownie bake!
Such eternal sadness echoes, life distracts with needs.
While the being burgeons forward, she fingers stone beads.

Buddhist practice she was taught, to count the beads pushed by;
Also, how to get your hippie file from the FBI.
Join the Peace Corps, block a tree-fall, organize a protest.
Make a dandelion crown, let out all that is suppressed!

Chant a marijuana slogan, paint a unicorn;
Calculate your horoscope, what time were you born?
'*Bread*' is money, '*bag*' is interest, '*groove*' is to enjoy.
Rap or split, turn on or trip, but do not dare destroy.

How to run a shared-house meeting; yoga salutation.
Saying no to "I will go" to her matriculation.
Changing oil in yonder bus, first take off the flowered shirt,
Later on's the time to play, and roll around in dirt.

Tie-dye clothing: add some fringe, bright color is the best!
Hitchhike out to California; save a robin's nest.
Grow an avocado seed: for nothing goes to waste.
Give her means to charity for she has been so graced.

Then grow up and bypass sixty, life slows down to zero.
Now's the time to sit and think of really, who's her hero?
Makes no diff'rence, it's been done, karma's a revoker.
How much she has or just how little: life is a provoker.

Never the Same

From second to second and place to place,
Ever the newness we all face.
Adapt and adjust, revise and amend,
Be ready for any straight arrow to bend.
When climbing a mountain and viewing a crater,
Think what could happen just one second later.
We drive every day and face bumps in the road;
Our brain runs the car, the car carries the load.
Is the load heavy, distracting or boring?
How many factions of mind now are warring?
One thing is certain with no one to blame:
Life is what is then, but never the same.

Power

A thousand ways we're vulnerable
Through skin and tears and taste,
A lifetime's lesson don't enable
Forgetfulness: a waste.
Repetition of the learning
'Til it fits together.
Working hard and always earning,
All despite the weather.

Mystery Enigma

Life's an unknown riddle.
Twixt animals with wee small brains
And brainless plants and trees,
Here we are stuck in the middle,
Without guarantees.

Animals don't have a brain
That makes them ask the "whys."
They don't tend to analyze
The millions of their tries,
Resulting in their prolonged lives.

Food is there or it is not
Shelter happens too.
Their instinct tells them how to live
For them there's no 'untrue.'

So thinking's the dilemma?
A constant dark umbrella,
That keeps the answers we all seek,
Bubbling by in yonder creek,
Never giving us a peek
of
WHY?

ABSENTEE MUSE

The dawn breaks over the eastern sky.
I lie here, just awake.
I couldn't write a poem today,
For anybody's sake.

The colors sparkle with the dew;
The clouds both gold and pink.
Cannot move to find the pen,
Don't want to even blink.

Laughter is a memory
Oldness changes all
No one knows when they'll get there
Each will hear the call
Lone tree sees itself, not more
In reflection near the shore
Nothing real except perception
Ends with selfish introspection
Sense with feelings, thoughts, volition
Self advances toward ambition

BIRTHDAYS

"It's my birthday," she said, as she bought a small cake.
Her companion was parked in the camp by the lake.
A tear rolling down 'cause her life was so broken,
Could not match the pain of the words she had spoken.

She'd reached 65, left abuse and her home.
Wasn't wont to be homeless or quite so alone.
Lived a close family life, then moved on to a sect,
Having no earthly concept how that would affect.

The word 'karma' kept ringing a tone in her mind,
Along with the hope that some love she would find.
Unaided, forlornly she'd bought her own cake.
And ate it alone, in the camp by the lake.

Grandparent Joy

Oh the utter delight - of seeing your grandbaby smile!
Oh the beautiful sight - of eyes peering out with no guile.

Oh the softest of skin - so pink, warm and new;
Oh the tiniest chin - eyes between light and dark blue.

Oh the squirms and the coos - wriggling body so small,
The arms fly in every direction.

A new life is happily born to the world,
All she needs is a parent's protection.

A 68th Spring

Spring comes rushing in,
Colors light and bold.
Trees and bushes spouting color,
Soon they will grow old.

Time is birth and death is life;
Nothing stays the same.
Beauty fades after it's found;
The eyes likewise will wane.

Blossoms go from pink to brown;
Everything soon dies.
But look around, a new plant blooms;
Existence has no guise.

Puff's Land

Light green, dark green,
every green I know.
Pink, peach and purple,
red-topped trees aglow.
Color deep is everywhere,
south or west or east.
Flowers crowd the landscape,
for the eyes: a feast!

Waves are crashing in the ocean, hurricane result.
Sunsets: orange and gold and silver, psyche doth exult.
Green-clad cliffs with waterfalls,
rainbows here and there,
Silver sea at sunset,
with a golden glare.

Can you hear it? Can you smell it?
Can you see perfection?
Tropical Kauai:
Bali Hai reflection.
Sun drops down beneath horizon,
camera at the ready.
Take a breath of purest beauty,
life shifts more toward steady.

Every year my soul comes home,
pressures seem to cease.
Sustenance to keep on going,
knowing there is peace.

West Coast Train Travel

Fields of green, fields of brown, swiftly moving by;
Lettuce and there's artichokes! Rows and rows of - something...
Gentle sways, the train moves on, ever newer sights,
Junk yards, backyards, shipyards - miles and miles of dumping.

Hills were green, last I saw, now they're brown and crusty;
Rivers, creeks, knolls and valleys, irrigation ditches.
Workers labor over yonder, now they've stopped for lunch,
Miles and miles of open land, see our country's riches.

Sleeping car and dining car but I sat in the lounge.
People talking, children walking, readers, eaters, sleepers;
Some on I pads, some with cameras, some stare out the window.
Sleep compartment, dining ritual, some seats sure are cheaper.

Lots of people, pinging info, in a rural setting;
Gismos, systems, all comes with us: train a big transmitter.
Older couple, from Australia, playing cards on deck;
Mother with a child in tow, next to her a knitter.

Next stop, who knows where or when, and then, what does it matter?
There's a house, and there's a tractor, who knows who's the owner?
Open sight, from a great height, peek into a lifestyle,
Travel's not a thing for those that like to be a loner.

Oil fields, oak trees, graveyards, farmsteads, everyone surviving;
Palm trees, wood stacks, storage buildings, horses eating yonder:
Mankind makes its mark on earth, yet nature's ever-present.
Travel slowly, watch the scene; for those who like to wander.

Then it's over, there you are: your relative is waiting.
Solid ground, still and present, what is different here?
Life's the same for all the people, all is a relating.
People, houses, life ongoing: just what you hold dear.

Waiting for the Train

Sitting in the Amtrak lounge, here in Union Station.
Folks of all sorts wait together, sampling of our nation.
People read, stare out the window,
old folks sit and watch the telly.
Someone reaches for a pastry, new mom pats her belly.

Lady counts her bills, sighs loudly; young girl thumbs her phone.
People talk, but not too many, everyone alone.
Station lady calls for singles, fits them on the tram.
Kids are antsy, squirming, dancing, hanging onto Gram.

Feel like crying, much good-byeing, everyone is leaving.
Deep inside my tears have dried but outside I am grieving.
Learned it fully years ago that there's an end to life.
I consider this one question, why is there so much strife?

KARMA

(to the tune *Tzena Tzena*)

Karma karma karma karma
You will get it back someday so watch!
Watch what you say!

Karma karma karma karma
Ev'rything you do comes back so watch!
Watch what you do.

In Flight to Oregon

99 below us,

and Shasta to the right.

Alcohol and ear plugs,

no sleep on the flight.

Cliffs and ranges, ridges, rivers,

over there a lake.

Farms and dams and towns and cities,

man his mark did make.

All those houses, all those cities,

all in just one state.

Multiply the many numbers,

how does it equate?

Somehow there along life's way

we figured that we should

Be responsible for all:

yeah, as if we could!

This peak south and that peak north,

and three more over there.

Dropping through the Portland clouds,

prop plane in midair.

Gazing outward, downward, upward,

through the tiny pane.

Mother Earth is getting closer,

wet with recent rain.

SEPARATENESS

That is them and this is me:
separate to infinity.
Elements the same at base,
all with a different face.
Different, same, who's to blame;
nothing is the same.
Missing atoms in the brain,
so that god could claim:
All is one in separateness.
not together, that's my guess.

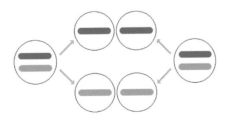

WHAT

What I didn't know then, I surely know now.
What I don't know now: the answer to "how?"
What I will know - gee, that's not up to me;
A leaf in the wind, but one that can see.

MEDITATION

Scintillating web of healing, made of whitest light.
Sparkling points of light revealing each man's inner sight.

Whispered prayers and meditations join the lighted course.
Miracles and revelations from the holy source.

In the light above my head are pictured those in need.
Up and out the healings spread where 'ere the light streams lead.

Joined by saints and holy ones and heavenly hierarch,
Brighter than a thousand suns the light usurps the dark.

The spirit atom in our heart is filled with this pure light
From life we will not ere depart, we're imaged in its sight.

And every night at dusk we merge our light with this great stream.
Our souls with others thus converge in light, in god supreme.

Sometimes Always Never

Sometimes
is in between
Always
and
Never

Always
seems
Sometimes
way beyond
Never

Never
is
Always
way beyond
Sometimes

HERE THEN, OR THERE; OR WHERE IN BETWEEN?

WHAT IS EXACT AND WHAT DOES IT MEAN?

AS IF YOU COULD PIECE IT TOGETHER TO BUILD

WHATEVER THE MIND'S EYE KNOWS HOW TO BE WILLED.

SO LIFE IS A QUESTION, AN UNKNOWN EXISTENCE.

LIKEWISE OUR BEINGS, AN UNKNOWN CONSISTENCE.

WHO WANTS TO KNOW WHY? ARE THERE MORE THEN, THAN I?

TO SOMEHOW KNOW ALL OF IT BEFORE I DIE?

IT'S BUILT-IN: RESISTANCE, INSISTENCE, THE VOID.

WE TRY TO BE LOVING, BUT END UP ANNOYED.

THAT

Now that she's an oldish lady- - - -Thinks she's going to die:
All the time the brain is growing- - - -Still she's askin': "Why?"

Could live yet another thirty- - - -Forty, God forbid!
People do, and she eats well- - - -Oh, who's she trying to kid?

Death's ahead and no one knows- - - -Just how or when or why.
Why'd she not think of it before- - - -This knowing she will die?

Gemini's two minds are thinking- - - -Battling now for space.
In fact, it seems that there are more- - - -But this is not a race.

Could be all the extra time- - - -*(Extra time?)*

Time you got to think of things- - - -Instead of always doin'.
No more need to join the race of- - - -Constantly pursuin'.

Time was taken up before- - - - -With workin' out survival.
Keepin' track, learning more- - - - -All activities are vital.

But life is set, except for crises- - - - -Stuck in narrow fiscal band.
What you have is what you get- - - - -Not much can one command.

Will it ever matter that- - - - -we don't know the name of that:
That is most important?

THAT

WHO ARE WE?

Nothing is mine, not even me.
I'm no diff'rent from yonder tree.
Strong winds blow, to bend or break,
Deep inside there is that ache.

Why can't we know just why we're here?
Why is our purpose so unclear?
What use to us a breathtaking scene,
In book or in person or there on the screen?

To eat, reproduce, to work or resist,
With constant unknowing we must coexist,
Survival: is that it? Just staying alive?
Does this make it our choice:
to maintain or to thrive?

That brings us to choice,
What's the less of two evils?
What steers us away
from unceasing upheavals?
Karma or luck or some destined design?
We do have a choice, we could choose to resign.

CHOICE

Did we choose
Not to remember
That we chose to be born?
or
Did we not choose
To be born
And not remember?

What of choice
And even of remembrance
Is truly ours?

Do we own choice?
or
Does choice own us?

Who can remember?

DEPRESSION VENT

Depression billows up like clouds in darkened skies,

Obscuring life's sweet visions from her tearful eyes.

Sullen anger weighs its hands upon her breast,

In its fiery swirl and cackle is no rest.

Whose responsibility is this hampered life;

Filled with sudden anger, suffering and strife?

Surely it's not hers, how can it she accept?

She has no will: the universe doth lead her every step.

DRIVEN BY FEAR

(Why Get Up in the Morning?)

Body says: I have to pee.
Body says: I have to eat.
Body says: Can't be too cold.
Body says: Not too much heat.

Minutely messages force us to go
Onto a path that we don't even know.
Toward life and living – that is a built in.
Toward death and dying – that we feel guilt in.

Money, Honey?

I'm out of grub, you've lost your scratch,

We've run clean out of dough.

We exchanged all our wampum,

So now we must forego.

$

Our loot is gone, we have no bills,

We've run right out of cash.

We have no bread, our bucks are gone;

And empty is the stash.

$

From have to have-not we have wandered:

Spending, giving, living.

It's funny how our money's gone,

And life is not forgiving.

NOT DONE

Horrible feeling there's something he's missing.

He can't see it all.

He can't do it all.

Oblivion waiting around every moment.

He tries to feel tall.

Death makes him feel small.

Remembering all he's been through, and not:

His brain an experience melting pot.

Mortality sits on his shoulder and shouts:

Filling intention with pressure and doubts.

EVERYWHERE

IS

HERE

IS

THERE

IS

EVERYWHERE!

TWO WEARY FOLKS WENT UP INTO THE HILLS

Two weary folks went up into the hills,

Visiting friends, they brought all their ills;

Sadness and tension, anxiety and woe,

Spirits and manner were awfully low.

Tripping through the door with hardly a hello,

These two long lost comrades were not very mellow.

Friends took them in and cooked a big meal,

With loving intent, to serve and to heal.

Soon they were all four lost in their talk,

Interrupted now and then, by the baby's squawk.

Chatting and listening, discussing and more,

Thinking and musing, sprawled out on the floor.

Face to the fire, with pillows and juice,

Gradually sadness began to shake loose.

Sharing our trials, ideas and thoughts,

Talking of errors, successes and oughts.

Warm embers crackle, the two rose to go,

Feeling the warmth of the fireplace glow.

Warm and refreshed, they were feeling so light,

Ready for action, though so late at night.

They stepped out the door with more love in their heart,

Gratitude flowing, they moved to depart.

And so being thankful for friends who can share,

They now approach life with a little more care.

CHIROPRACTIC

Twisted spine or subluxation:
Are you misaligned?
Does your spine need palpitation?
Can you twist behind?

Chiros, they restabilize,
Make you more efficient.
You don't even realize
What has been deficient.

Twists and traumas, structure stress,
Accidents and repeat motion;
Your back may be quite a mess
Even from emotion.

Be more balanced. You'll live longer,
If your spine is straight.
Chiro makes you feel much stronger;
Orders metabolic state.

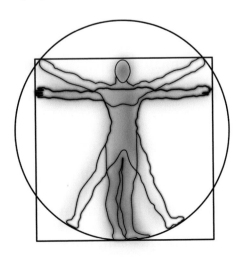

How Do I Judge Thee?
Let Me Count the Ways...

I sit in judgment of thy face, I note its every trait.

I watch thy body, form and style. Thy hair I also rate.

I note thy clothes, the car thou drives; I wonder what thou'rt worth.

Hast thou in life more wealth than I? Or can I tell thy dearth?

I look for things especially that might be unlike me;

For who else could I judge thee by; for who else can I see?

I judge thy mind and look for signs to tell me of thy brains.

How much telepathy hast thou? How dost thou play life's games?

I judge thy virtues and thy good. Art thou as pure as I?

Dost thou a holy life embrace? How dost thou qualify?

There is no item that I miss, be it great or small.

Mine eyes do judge thee up and down, and form thee overall.

What vulgar, hateful sport is this, this game I always play.

To judge each one I come across, to silently inveigh.

Before I've even met the man, my wicked mind designs;

His every feature has been classed, my petty mind confines.

I know I have this mental match of judging every one.

It is no wonder that I feel no love from any one.

In judging others, I am judged; I open up the door.

Each time I judge another, I will be judged the more.

If only I could know of love, and in that love be sure;

To feel a real part of the plan, important and secure.

BEC-KEN GARDEN 2

Jasmine glory, scented heaven; bougainvillea too.
Cypress trees and pepper tree; bottlebrushes: two.

Doves beneath the orange tree, blue jays up above,
Nuthatch hops the trunk in front, hummingbirds I love.

Sparrows at the feeder, junco at the fountain,
Pink and purple soft petunias; left: Diablo mountain.

Rosemary and sunflower; in the garden: kale.
Artichokes, calendula: trimmed by unseen snail.

Sheets are drying in the breeze beneath the mighty oak
Holly, lily and tomato, it was there I woke:

In time to see the hawk, circling overhead.
Thought he'd land atop the pine tree; he flew off instead.

Red squirrel tries to reach the feeders, stymied every time.
Swinging ropes and catching latches thwart his every climb.

Likewise neighbor's yellow cat just cannot catch a break,
Hears my clapping, shouting, grumbling: does a double take.

Backyard, front yard, small town noises, far-off sound of train,
Book and glasses on the chaise are wet from last week's rain.

California, sunny realm, the weather nearly perfect.
Trees and bushes everywhere, the flowers grow unchecked.

Halleluiah! I must say, (I came from Buffalo.)
Treasuring the sweet warm weather, in my bungalow.

THE LIGHT

It was up on Deadman's Summit I first saw the light.
It shown down on Devil's Swamp on that October night.
I had come from Crystal Craig where life was pretty easy.
Now I'm here in Roving Meadow feeling pretty queasy.

That strange light I thought had gone but here it is again.
Standing now in Red Rock Canyon, quite a dry domain.
From the sky it comes down streaking, like a lightning bolt
And whenever I have seen it, gives me such a jolt!

Aspen Springs and Badger Pass and Echo Cave: 'twas there.
And on the Desert Island over by the Prickly Pear.
Lasts a second or a minute, I don't even know
Stand there fascinated by the eerie purple glow.

Sometimes yellow, sometimes green like at the Marshy Flat.
One time t'was a streaming rainbow: stunning image that.
I remember Granite Lake, the light was in the waters,
That's the time I went to visit my two pretty daughters.

Pebble Creek it seemed to bend, flashing in the forest.
Like a thousand pretty flowers from the local florist.
No one else has ever seen it, think I'm pretty mad.
Words can't do it justice, makes me pretty sad.

Can't explain it, can't left-brain it, cannot clarify.
Others think it strange and scary, 'odd' doth terrify.
It's external. Or internal? Happens just to me.
Inner life or outer life: only I can see.

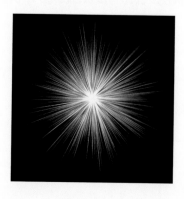

Out the Window of the Train

Pipes and pallets, blocks of concrete, boxes rotting in the dirt.

Three old couches, shiny bottles, wrinkled flowered shirt.

Mattresses, red paper cups, tumbleweeds and blowing reeds:

All are littered by the tracks, showcasing man's needs.

Old man smoking, rusting fences, bicycle all bent;

Train rolls past and sees it all: America's lament.

Colorful graffiti, sprayed on with such a hope.

Or the loss of such a feeling, when one sees the scope.

Ticky-tacky matching houses, washtubs in the yard,

Stuff packed into every corner, proving life is hard.

Dirty creeks and broken shelving, age-old grocery cart.

Empty warehouse, dusty crating through which rabbits dart.

Used-cars, used-homes, lifetimes of old grimy junk:

Random placement 'mongst dead grasses - defines the term funk.

Each old item tells a story - globally personal.

Speaks in tongues the same for all – randomly universal.

She'll Be All Right When the Company Comes

Her mother died and she'd been raped twice;
But she'll be all right when the company comes.
Psychologist kissed her and husband stole her house;
But she'll be all right when the company comes.

Died on the table, doctor looking worried;
But she'll be all right when the company comes.
Caught up in a faction, escaped it one dark night;
But she'll be all right when the company comes.

Then her offspring hated her, husband wouldn't speak to her;
But she'll be all right when the company comes.
Tears and anger spill and mar her face.
But she'll be all right when the company comes.

Helplessness

Baby in an intersection.

H

Sneezes carry bad infection.

E

Carelessly the boxes stacked.

L

Don't know why computer's hacked.

P

One misstep upon the stair.

L

Attitude says "I don't care."

E

Broken body, broken spirit.

S

We eventually will fear it.

S

The Mockingbird

It used to be told of a young mockingbird
Who lived in my front yard tree.
How he'd sing in the night, in the morn, in the eve.
Telling all of the joy to fly free.

All the birds all around could respond to his sound
But the calls came too many and fast.
He had copied the tunes of the neighboring flocks
And kept chirping till they had all passed.

Then today as I raked up the leaves and debris
'Neath the mulberry front yard tree,
Lay the feathers white, never more for flight,
Now the bird's tune a memory.

NEW YORK STATE: MAY 8TH

Fifty years ago today, I made a decision,
Based on certain factors that assaulted my vision.
Spring had sprung, the air was warm and daffodils were blooming:
So very long I'd waited for that delicate perfuming.

But everything was blanketed in three inches of snow!
I said right then, "I'm out of here!" I really had to go.
Who chooses life where winter temps last more than half a year?
A warmer clime for me was one thing that was very clear.

So goodbye coldness, goodbye snow and let's escape dark clouds.
I'd rather live with warmer air in spite of all the crowds.
I don't know how, I don't know when, but I am going west:
Some place where the weather doesn't keep me so distressed.

I said goodbye and took a flight, I've been here ever since;
A warmer spot where freezing air will never make me wince.

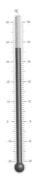

FLICKERING MOSCATO

Flickering candle on restaurant table, watching the pattern of flickers;
Sipping Moscato and waiting for partner, in walks a lady in knickers.
She's given a flicker and orders Moscato, looking straight over at me,
And now comes the kicker:
    She's the image of me
       and anyone here would agree.

We stare for awhile with nary a smile, is this some kind of deceiving?
It's hard to relate, reconcile or explain, the mind seems to negate believing.
But here is a sibling, a daughter, a cousin: a relative that is for certain.
    A question, two questions, perplexing and vexing;
      like someone has pulled back a curtain.

She stands up first, pays her bill, then comes over, and I looking up stare in shock;
Her eyes, nose and mouth are exactly like mine and abruptly I can't seem to talk.
Her eyes dark and deep that now seem to weep
    Make her face full of tension and sadness.
      Staring into her face, I can't stop my gape,
        my psyche trips slowly toward madness.

"What's your name?" her voice cracks, and that's when I notice:
    her cheek has a tiny red scar.
Stick to facts, my mind screams,
    this person and I are both in the same Concord bar.

The rain in the headlights ten feet out the window, show me that my partner is here.
Who is she, who am I, what's happening here, and how to explain the vague fear?

She turns then to leave and I've not said a word, my partner is coming this way.
Can he see her or she him as they pass, can he hear that I've called her to stay?

Knowing (or not)

We wish we were just *somewhere else*
With this or that great feature.
To avoid the ignorance
Of us:
the human creature!

To know
that you don't know
what you need to know
in order to

survive

seems an essential missing point
to both
the creator and the created.

Instead:
It's miss or miss
(rarely a 'hit')
Forever.
Until death:
Which is frequently painful.

So.
Take another

deep breath

(What else can you do?)

Where've YOU Been?

Ventura has rockslides and Mammoth has crags,
DC's a plethora of flapping flags.
Kauai is gorgeous: all colors abound,
LA is warm but with wall-to-wall sound.

Florida's muggy and Tucson is hot,
Southwest has cactus and that's all they got.
Vegas is crowded and stupid and phony.
Buffalo's known for its ham and baloney.

State parks and federal throughout the nation.
Landmasses beautiful: inspiring elation.
Crossed the Atlantic a few times at least,
Way prefer west but was born in the east.

Germany's cold but the castles are sumptuous,
France is quite poor but the food there is scrumptious!
Greece is aglitter with white against blue:
Sky blue and Sea blue compete for the view.

Mexico's poorest are three-year-olds pleading,
Spain's bulls are wounded and race around bleeding.
All of these places I've been to and more,
All of these things I can truly speak for.

Ithaca College gave me a free ride.
I was still there when I first 'came a bride.
Moved then to Philly and then overseas;
I'm just turned twenty a/broad with unease.

Alps are my favorite – three countries have them.
Ecstasy, wonder: the facets of Alp gem.

Vast are the distances, rugged the edges, Viewed from
a cave 'neath some dangerous ledges.

Huntington saw life through the out-house door,
Life without power – a "new" to explore.
Poverty level but knowing it not.
One thing, then 'nother, all with not-a-lot.

The Peace Bridge: crossed often, no boats going under;
So frequent the visits: the Falls was no wonder.
Grand Canyon and Yellowstone, Smokies, Yosemite.
Canada, Barbados, and last New York City.

Places – all over – and life is the same.
Everything has just its place and its name
No matter the address, the newness is craved.
There's also the bounty from things that are braved.

Niagara Falls

Expectation Recipe

(Ingredients: use matter)

expectation = 1 oz of security

security = 2 oz lack of suddenness

suddenlessness = 3 oz no fear

no fear = 4 oz tranquility

tranquility = 5 oz no motion

no motion = 6 oz death

death = 7 oz end-of-life

end-of-life = 8 oz unknown

unknown = 1/2 pound of

"what does it matter?"

Contra Costa Birding

Sixteen bird types I've had the luck to see,
Out here in Concord, not far from the sea.
Came home from teaching, opened the car door;
Greeted by a screeching, sounded like a war!
Sparrows, finches, phoebes darting here and there
Squawking to the universe: "Cooper's hawk: beware!"
Ran to get the camera, didn't faze the hawk,
She looked down and all around, watched me as I walked.
Soon she tired, flapped her wings, flew across the street,
Got my shots, put food away, had a bite to eat.
Filled the back yard feeders with the suet, seeds and thistle,
Just in time to hear the cedar waxwing's well-known whistle.
In the winter, robins flock, and raven's sit on fence posts.
Waiting for a chance to fly off with leftover jam toasts.
Nuthatch hopping down the trunk, towhees down below,
In the neighbor's redwood sits the ever-present crow.
Dark eyed junco's unafraid of little Tommy titmouse,
Those are just a few of feathered friends who stop at this house.
At the shore on Sunday last, the mallards did abound.
Also, spotted sandpipers who ran along the ground.
On the buoy sat the gulls and overhead a pelican.
Sights and sounds of all the birds: that's what makes me well again.

Full Openness

It happens in the bathroom

With the toilet seat

It happens at the front door

Loved ones that we greet

It happens at the window

When we need a breeze

It happens at the nightstand drawer

When we have a sneeze

It happens in the garage

When we stack the lumber

It happens in our beds each day

When we wake from slumber

It happens in conditioned minds

When we see anew

When we take away the blinds

Of limited review

Hidden Importances

Of course there is gardening.

And there is taking pictures.

And there is nothing like scenic Kauai.

Flowers and trees in amazing spring bloom.

And there are my interesting poems.

And now in my life is sweet Josie Grace

Who is captivating as a baby can possibly be.

But what is Important with a capital I,

And as beautiful as an ocean sunset,

Much closer to my heart than my heart:

(And there is only one of this person)

My wonderful daughter whom I love so much!

Head Full of Heartbeat

Bury Her Deep Beneath Sequoia Trees

Pounding, pulsing: deep inside her head;
  Signals to the brain that she is sure not dead.
    Abandonment problems in the ancestral line:
      Husbands-leaving-wives becomes the life baseline.
Her Grandpa left her Grandma - when her Momma was two.
  Her Grandpa left her Grandma on the other side too.
    Both parents brought up by quite dominant women,
      Who'd been left to live a life that they could barely learn to swim in.
Both deserted mothers, went back to live with theirs,
  Two strong women, thusly, raised the grandchild-heirs.
    Her Mom was one of those offspring, indeed,
      She lived in the room of her grandfather's seed.
She came from marital problems too -
  Her father left her mother with their daughters: two.
    They got back together but the damage was done,
      She became the end result of reconciliation.
Her daughter's teenage years surely were torn asunder
  By a marriage that was lost and thus bereft of thunder.
    Three years of no intimacy, words were barely spoken,
      This left a loneliness, a soul was heartbroken.
Most daughters favored fathers at this adolescent stage,
  Which causes them to truly, from their mothers, disengage.
    Naiveté caused nightly tears and then came resignation,
      She always hoped there could be so much more to a relation.
With so much loss and facing death, what is a mom to do?
  There has been oh so much she's had to just eschew.
    Soon are gone the days of doubt with every breath she breathes,
      She'll breathe the scent of fallen leaves beneath Sequoia trees.

Aging Gracefully

No!
I am not going to age gracefully!
There's still a LOT that I haven't

Done, Experienced, Loved, Learned, Seen

And why would
THE SPIRIT OF ADVENTURE
and
THE DESIRE TO LEARN
have been inborn in us
if we are going to

die

And lose it all to the great
UNKNOWN

Which is scary; and frankly,
UNKNOWN!

Wanting

It isn't what I want.......then......I get the thing I want,
but,
It isn't what I want........so.........what is it that I want?

Sonnet to the Fourth of July

💙 9:33 AM

I just LOVE the Fourth of July: everything about it!
People celebrating freedom, what could be more stirring?
Singing, watching fireworks, saying "Yes! I am so proud."
Differences are quite diminished; feeling: reassuring.

💙 11:33 AM

People singing all together, dressed in country's colors,
Walking in a town parade: anyone can march.
I've got my deal, you've got yours, together we exist.
Hand in hand we jointly triumph, through the balloon arch.

💙 9:33 AM

Trumpets blaring, dark skies bursting, we remember freedom.
Independence. Some don't have it, we have been so blessed.
Celebrate emancipation, kiss your kids and friends.
Red and white and blue our colors, U.S. is the best!

💙 11:33 AM

Thanks we give for this great feeling: safety and protection.
For our country - its ideals: we have such great affection.

States

allegation, agitation, altercation, aggravation
defamation, desolation, desperation, devastation
confrontation, complication, condemnation, confiscation
inflammation, isolation, infestation, irritation
Tired yet?
infiltration, indignation, mutilation, molestation
provocation, refutation, violation, tribulation
segregation, separation, sequestration, termination
provocation, usurpation, indignation, resignation
OK then, how about:
fabrication, inundation, exploitation, exhortation
aberration, consternation, conflagration, deportation
States of being in our nation?
strangulation, obfuscation, malformation, machination
limitation, isolation, irritation, laceration
hesitation, domination, deviation, dislocation
cancellation, amputation, accusation, resignation
Negativation?

Bec-Ken Garden

Gladiola and begonia, poppy, iris, marigold;
Bee balm, pansy and nasturtium: gorgeous to behold.
Barrel cactus, calla lily by the scented rose.
Giant jasmine bushes blooming: sugar for the nose.

Dahlia and geranium: pink and red and white.
Two big giant rhododendrons make a stunning sight.
Cannas in the green pot, pink petunia draping;
Brimming pots of white alyssum, patio reshaping.

Jasmine glory, scented heaven; bougainvillea too.
Cypress trees and pepper tree; bottlebrushes: two.
Doves beneath the orange tree, blue jays up above,
Nuthatch hops the trunk in front, hummingbirds we love.

Sparrows at the feeder, junco at the fountain,
Pink and purple soft petunias; left: Diablo Mountain.
Rosemary and sunflower; in the garden: kale.
Artichokes, calendula: trimmed by unseen snail.

Sheets are drying in the breeze beneath the mighty oak.
Holly, lily and tomato, it was there we woke.
Just in time to see the hawk, circling overhead.
Thought he'd land atop the pine tree; he flew off instead.

Red squirrel tries to reach the feeders, stymied every time.
Swinging ropes and catching latches thwart his every climb.
Likewise neighbor's yellow cat just cannot catch a break,
Hears my clapping, shouting, grumbling: does a double take.

Backyard, front yard, small town noises, far-off sound of train.
Book and glasses on the chaise are wet from last night's rain.

WAKE UP IN YOSEMITE

There's a songbird in the forest and a chirper to the right;
Distant roar of waterfalls; tent walls getting bright.
Warm and snug inside the bag but nose is out and cold.
Body has to go again: says I'm getting old.

Quickly slip on pants and shoes, hooded jacket too.
Quietly unzip the tent flap, heading toward the loo.
Suddenly a banging, yelling – not too far away.
People scaring yellow* bear! How to start the day!
(color of tag on bear's ear)

Goodnight Mammoth

The crag is the last one to bid sun good-night.
The shadows have crept east to west, left to right.
The air is now cooler, the forest is still.
The full moon now creeps over yonder hill.

A day of adventure, a memory now.
One after another, the spoken word, "Wow!"
The canoe on the lake and the fisherman's take,
The camera ready – a picture to make.

A Lake Called George

Whispers of the stalwart pines, across the lake of lapping shores;

Sits the yonder crag called Crystal, from which rushing water pours.

High atop the great Sierras, eastern snow-capped ranges wander.

Rock-strewn valleys, red-hued cliffs: worth the time to sit and ponder.

Grasses cling to stony ledges, chipmunks scurry o'er the boulder.

Giant ants search here and there, gnarled tree against my shoulder.

Breathe it in and listen well, fill the mem'ry with the sight.

Take it back to daily workplace, in the heart: nature's delight.

Giant Sequoias

Calaveras Big Trees State Park seems innocuous.
But stand beneath the great Sequoia: it's incredulous!
Gasps of "WOW!" erupt from tourists: so hard to believe.
Trunks of up to thirty feet wide, so hard to conceive.

Only here in California do these big trees grow.
Biggest trees on this green earth, nothing apropos.
Awe and reverence, even teardrops, fill the mind with wonder,
Beauty and immensity; scary: just like thunder!

Who are we, so small and frail, and younger than the ages?
These big trees have been around since hist'ry wrote its pages.
Save your pennies, research nature, travel far and wide.
Find things beautiful, inspiring; get yourself outside!

Games of the Fifties

We played ping pong in the basement and jumped pogo sticks outside.
Bow and arrows shot at targets, baseballs smacked out in the street.
Racing to the playground, our bikes flew like the wind;
Faster, faster, chase that cowboy! Then play hide and seek.
Scrabble, Boggle, Memory, Dominoes and Jenga,
Rummy played with Nana as the freight trains all went by.
Family Night we all had candy, M&Ms the best!
Chutes and Ladders: that was fast but longest was Monopoly.
My brother going wacko when he lost three times to Rack-O.
You could use psychology and get him every time.
Jigsaw puzzles, crossword puzzles, later on Sudoku;
Jarts, croquet and badminton, oh winning was sublime!

Silence

I walked in front of the visitor center in the middle of Wyoming.
There is where I found it lodging, after a long search.
I popped my ears just to make sure, but it was truly there:
Not a single sound is heard, on my rocky perch.
Not the rustle of a leaf, not a voice or car or bird,
Not the wind and not the weather: silence is the consequence.
><
Ears are ringing, hear the heartbeat, jacket rustles so.
No such things as perfect silence: life's the subsequence.

Lighted Sight

I am as a blind man: groping for the truth.
I'm feeling with hands that transmit a suggestion.
There is a perception of knowing in this,
A hint of the path,
But not sight.

        I struggle to know and to answer the queries,
            I listen and taste, I inhale and I touch.
            And all this gives me is a part of the whole;
            A sensual truth,
        But not light.

I peel off the layers of incorrect wisdom,
Seeking to know what's inside.
The skins of the dream are revealed in a shadow,
From blackness to grey,
But not white.

        Of wrong I learn well, through pain and disease;
            I narrow the vast field of untruth and of evil.
            Each day I know more of the wrong in the world
            Of ill I know much,
        But not right.

A moment reveals now the real side of life.
A light is turned on for a second
The brief glimpse of union stays on in the mind
A memory true,
But not bright.

        I yearn for the time and the season of birth
            When trials will be overcome.
            When victory in darkness will turn into light
            And man in his mind
        Will have sight.

INDOCTRINATION

DOCTRINED-IN BY PARENTING
DOCTRINED-IN BY TEACHING
DOCTRINED-IN: SOCIETY
DOCTRINED-IN BY PREACHING
WHAT THOUGHTS THEN ARE TRULY OURS?
WHAT'S 'ORIGINAL?'
PATHWAYS SHOOTING THROUGH THE BRAIN
NARROW BRIDGES TO IT ALL

MEANING

Looking for significance in this green leaf or that.
Must be certain reasons why a person comes to bat.

Why did that small circumstance occur in just that way?
Coinciding universal forces are at play?

Cannot be that there is just no simple explanation;
Will we know before that day of final exhalation?

 Poverty

There's a horrible, sinking fear
When you live in poverty.
There's no such thing as cheer
In the land of paucity.

Knawing feelings of a danger
Just around the corner.
Everyone's a total stranger,
You end up a mourner.

Anxious and uneasy:
Can't see what's not known.
Sometimes feeling queasy,
Nothing to postpone.

RECURRING DREAM

Pass out. Sleep. Underwater.

In the pool. Save my daughter.

Cannot take a breath.

Where's the air? Way up there.

O my God! And I am bare!

Fear of certain death.

Wake up then. Look around.

Consciousness has justly found

Me in my warm bed.

Where was I or who was I?

What is real and what's a lie?

All that's left is dread.

Plant Diagnostic Workshop

Gardeners are all assembled, trying to find the cure.

Splotchy leaves and yellowed veins: no one's really sure.

How much water? How's the soil? Does it grow in sun?

Master Gardeners check their workbooks. Are we having fun?

Arrangement

Structure, manner, shape or form;
model, method to perform.
Type or style, a distinct nature,
compared to the norm.

What configuration or procedure
do we choose to mold?
Is appearance all external?
What then do we hold?

Anger forbidden, emotions well hidden:
so later on
The feelings are missing.

Enter religion, with past lives and karma:
so later on
Emotions dismissing.

Beeping Lights in the Middle of the Night

Smoke detector in the bedroom, 'nother in the hall;
Glowing time on dresser seen in mirror on the wall.
Red TV light shows its power, blue is on the cord strip;
Phone by bed and I-pad chirps, sleep has lost its grip.

    Go to bed in darkness?

      No -

        Not

          Quite

Every thirty seconds there's a
    flash of *light*

FLYING FIRST CLASS

We have all this r o o m - - - We have all this s p a c e
And Yippie! It is
First Class!

We are on the move - - - Get in camera groove
And Yippie! I'm in
First Class!

Food and drinks are free - - - Hot towels with the tea
And Yippie! There is
First Class!

Frank's Famous Hot Dogs

Kraut dog, bacon dog, corn dog, chili dog - that is what you'll get,
Unless you order garden burger - appetite whet yet?
Sign says "I'm a wiener," get it? Dogs with Cajun, turkey, cheese;
Monster burgers, fried zucchini - nothing here Chinese.
Chili-cheese-fries, mini-burgers, sundaes, cones and floats.
Something here for everyone: grub that floats your boats.
Come and get it, weekly specials, **Famous Franks in SLO.**
Red and white umbrellas draw you - you have got to go!

Constant Change

…constant: change…
…constant; change…
Constant. Change.
…constant, change…
…constant change…

Rainbows

Rainbow presence means: the sun is at your back.
Gotta know this fact if you want to keep track.
There's a price for pleasure and it always is exact.
Don't want to be moaning over all that you will lack.

LONE DAFFODIL

Oh pretty daffodil, your petals so bright.

Deep inhalation, deep yellow light;

Intricate tenderness, soft petal folds,

Joy to the soul from your velvety golds.

Silent and welcome, you herald a spring

Freedom from bitter, the promise you bring.

You vs. frost equals man vs. life,

Maintaining reason throughout all the strife.

PURPOSE

The meaning of life is pondered intensely, one searches for a purpose.

Or one performs the tasks of living and then sees only surface.

Yet always the question of "What is next?" plays havoc with the mind.

Now old and tired with little hope – some perfect fit to find.

But can this attitude be changed? Is thought itself the cause?

Relentless seconds all tick by and we can never pause.

Night after night we toss pillows aside.
Into our bed then we silently slide.
Lights still ablaze, the door open wide:
Close the eyes - Let it slide
Lose the fear - Let it ride.
Relax the shoulders, let go the knees.
Set mind adrift, let go wanting-to-please.
How do we know what the mind thinks it sees?
Who is it? Where am I? Why question why?
Our reach can't quite make it to "pie-in-the-sky."
An O and a K both together make sense;
And life's not a game played at someone's expense.

comparing

comparing and ordering … the haves and have-nots;
which one am I … connect the dots.
live up to a standard … and follow the rules
that is, assuming … you've been given the tools
oh yeah, there's religion … the answer to all
what if you don't hear … the duplicitous call
it's inborn: this feeling … to want to have more
so why is it wrong … this needing the score

Happy Accident

Life's a happy accident
Following an unknown path.
Attitude gives life it's bent:
Calm response or loosened wrath.
Why use 'happy' you may ask?
When outcomes are unknown?
Perhaps that is our fated task:
Think happy when your cover's blown.
Wait and see or do and move.
Both ways can seem to be,
How one stays within the groove.
Decode bad memory.

Who controls the feeling-thought?
How much of it is what we're taught?

TRAIN TRAVEL

House after house and street after street,
Ball fields and churches and fields full of wheat.
Oil refineries, stock cars and drums:
All passes by as the train engine hums.

Lounge car is empty except for a hat:
Left on the seat edge where somebody sat.
Wide-brimmed and tan with a colorful tassel,
On the back edge is the print of a castle.

Internet's out but cameras still work.
Eating your lunch when the train's sudden jerk
Dumps your lunch in your lap, your drink on the floor;
But here's the attendant to bring you some more.

Walk down the aisle, your balance will wobble.
Dining car fancy, except folks who gobble.
Sitting with strangers, a crap shoot of luck;
Placed with an old man who's got lots of pluck.

Hour after hour as the coast rushes by,
Town after town with the landscape so dry.
Sound of the whistle around every curve,
There by the mountain, a nature preserve.

Closer to midnight the train starts to slow,
Here is the stop point, the town where you go.
Step off in darkness, your good friend is there.
Body still moving, the old mal de mer.

WHAT IF, SUDDENLY, THERE ARE NO WALLS

You can see him puffin' on his pipe,
Just a narrow wall away from you.
He can see you reading on the john,
Jotting down a crossword puzzle clue.
The heat kicks on and then you have to leave.
Going to the Home Depot for some wood.
To build a higher fence because the neighbor's
light shines in your rooms,
which isn't good.
But suddenly there are no walls and clearly
There he sits in front of his TV.
There are no walls, not even fences.
ALL Is there:
his shorts are open: so carefree!
But he sees me as well
and there we are:
All stunned, defensive, wary and unsure.
And then we see the others everywhere,
With nothing twixt us . . . . . nothing to obscure.
A great big WE - just you and me
and nothing
separates.
So are we strangers – you and me?
We're all the same – we're in this boat
Together - Closer than ever,
but all is new.
For NOW we all must find another way to live:
among, assembled, close;
For nothing stands between the human beings,
And life has gone from personal to gross.

Sciatica

The first doctor said
"Don't lie on the couch."
The second doctor said
"Does this cause an 'ouch?'"
The third doctor said
"Try this for awhile"
The fourth doctor said,
"It's not in your file…?"
The fifth doctor said
"Well, here's your diagnosis…"
The sixth doctor didn't say
"Well, here's your prognosis…"
And that's because, to tell the truth
Meant that his colleagues had no proof.

Paranoia

Terror, fear:
Lack of cheer.
Mistrust, dread;
Been mislead?
Worry, panic,
Being manic?
Trepidation,
Agitation.
Apprehension,
Hypertension.
Mitigation:
Knowing
Brain is altered.
(Can we be paranoid of being paranoid?)

SECOND TRIP DOWN COAST CA

Fields of green, fields of brown, swiftly moving by;
Lettuce and there's artichokes! Rows and rows of something...
Gentle sways, the train moves on, ever newer sights,
Junk yards, backyards, shipyards - miles and miles of dumping.
Hills were green, last I saw, now they're brown and crusty;
Rivers, creeks, knolls and valleys, irrigation ditches.
Workers labor over yonder, now they've stopped for lunch,
Miles and miles of open land, see our country's riches.
Sleeping car and dining car, but I sat in the lounge,
People talking, children walking, readers, eaters, sleepers;
Some on I-pads, some with cameras, some stare out the window.
Sleep compartment, dining ritual, some seats sure are cheaper.
Lots of people, pinging info, in a rural setting;
Gismos, systems, all comes with us: train a big transmitter.
Older couple, from Australia, playing cards on deck;
Mother with a child in tow, next to her a knitter.
Next stop, who knows where or when, and then, what does it matter?
There's a house, and there's a tractor, who knows who's the owner?
Open sight, from a great height, peek into a lifestyle,
Travel's not a thing for those that like to be a loner.
Oil fields, oak trees, graveyards, farmsteads, everyone surviving;
Palm trees, wood stacks, storage buildings, horses eating yonder:
Mankind makes its mark on earth, yet nature's ever-present.
Travel slowly, watch the scene; for those who like to wander.
Then it's over, there you are: your relative is waiting.
Solid ground, still and present, what is different here?
Life's the same for all the people, all is a relating.
People, houses, life ongoing: just what you hold dear.

Kitty, Kitty

Kitty, kitty how I love you,
How you have the softest fur.
Kitty, kitty how I love you,
How you have the sweetest purr.
Chasing after blue jays, resting on the green chaise;
Kitty, kitty how I love you
You make things secure.

APPEARANCES

You have one set of clothes for the garden
You have one set of clothes for work
You have one set of clothes for the farmer's market
And boy, are you such a jerk.
You assume someone cares, you assume someone sees
You assume you have outward worth.
While living inside is a little voice
That tells you, you're a jerk.

To Mothers Way Back

Hey Mom and Gram, what was life like for you?
Did you suffer alone, did you think, "What's the use?"
Did you have to know why, did you wonder who's "I"?
Did you want to know more, or to even the score?
Did you think about "How?" Did you ever say, "Wow!"
Did you worry or fret; with yourself make a bet?
Did you think about death, did you do yoga breath?
Did you find you could trust, a life that's not just?

TO ESCAPE

Have you been   in a marriage   where you had **TO ESCAPE** In a clunker of a camper - leaving everything behind?
(To keep your sanity?)
Have you been   in a cult   where you had **TO ESCAPE** In the middle of the night - leaving everything behind?
(Like your insanity?)
Have you been   in a dream   where you had **TO ESCAPE** The pursuer - but the locks on the doors - were all broken?
(Is life all inanity?)
Have you been   in a body   where you had **TO ESCAPE** From the pain   of an injury, and 'hope'   becomes 'heartbroken'?

(Is life pro-humanity?)

WAITING

To wait is to stop,
There's nothing to do.
The timing's not yet,
At least not for you.

You sit and you think;
You're still and you wait.
You're waiting for what?
To merge with your fate?

If reason there is
To all things in life.
If timing of all
Is perfectly right,

Then why do we wait?
What for is this time,
When sitting in wait,
To make up a rhyme?

To wait is to give
Importance to that
Which lies just ahead
On life's moving track.

But all time is right,
And all time is good;
Time thoughtfully used
Is time understood.

So next time you wait,
Take the time to reflect:
That all time is now,
And now is perfect.

Sweet Robin

Sweet Robin
Thou remindeth me of times before,
When as a child I'd listen by the door,
At dusk when light was fading from the sky,
I'd glance and see you in the tree nearby.

Sweet Robin,
Every year you come again to sing,
O'er the fields the crystal notes will ring.
With your song a silent peace descends,
In the hours before the daylight ends.

Sweet Robin,
Angels nigh must use your sweet refrain,
To still our thoughts and fill with love again.
Our hearts, so hidden by our selfish ways,
So that we cannot feel the heart's light-rays.

Sweet Robin,
Life to life you sing to us at dusk,
Human heart cups fill with faith and trust
Sweet songs fill our hearing sense
Without which is no recompense.

SIGNS OF SPRING

What is all the noise that on the house the rain doth make?
Why comforts us: the gentle sound of dripping from the eaves?
Why is it from the rain in spring we thus our pleasures take?
What hope is there in melting snow and last year's crumbled leaves?

End of May, the garden's in,
The little seedlings sprout;
Sweet spring scents waft gently by,
The lilacs have come out.

Twas but a week or so ago,
When it was cold and drear.
One wondered if the spring would come,
When *would* warm days be here?

The sun has dropped below the trees,
The birds increase their song.
The breeze has stopped, the trees are still,
It will be dark 'ere long.

The peepers start their nighttime cry,
The birds no longer sing.
The day has faded into night,
And winter into spring.

Signs of Life

The doctor held the instrument against my naked belly,
His other hand moved slowly with the tone-piece to his ear.
The silence of the tiny office sounded in my heart,
Gazing up in question for whatever he could hear.
>He moved the piece around a bit, his face revealed no sign,
>I watched him as I lay there, not without a little fear.
>Then suddenly he held it out, a different way, toward me,
>I saw the faintest half-hid smile around his eyes appear.
>My own heartbeat I heard with ease, resounding in the room;
>And then the faintest quickened pulse I heard, though not as clear.
A wave of something overpowered me, a rush of tiny chills,
The sound of life within my womb produced a veiled tear.
The one who grows within me now I will not take for granted,
It dwells now deep within my knowing, all life I will revere.

Rainy Spring

April rains that saturate the ground,

Dripping eaves in ceaseless splatter sound.

Puddles form and rivers cross the road,

Rushing waters stone and mud erode.

Peepers screaming, frenziedly they mate,

Soldier robins cock their heads and wait;

Multitudes of worms are all around,

Pushing through the surface of the ground.

Smells of rain-drenched, wormy, up-turned earth,

Mother nature waiting to give birth;

Trees in flower drop their swollen seeds,

Nature's embryos, each raindrop feeds.

Joyous days of spring have come at last,

All too soon for us they will have passed.

Accidents, 1976, Accidents?

Winter storm
  Ice and snow
    Drive to work
     Curvy Road
      Make the curve
       Make the curve?
Slippery, skidding, turning, screaming: CRASH!

Can't believe it
  How'd it happen?
   Wasn't speeding
    Wasn't braking
     You all right?
      Yes you are
Call my husband, call the boss, call policeman, call a friend.

Here's the cop
  Here's the wrecker
   Thirty dollars?!
    Gotta pay it
     Fill out forms
      No insurance
Neck is hurting, body shocked, home and safe now, bed is warm.

Spoken Tokens

Two Old Fogies

By
Becky Askin

Written from 2011-2012
Lake Jackson, Virginia
and
Concord, California

Two old fogies gazin' at the lake.
Watching as the eagle dives and grabs his take.
Follow with the camera, snap the bird in flight.
All in all a peaceful time and a thrilling sight.
Along comes the engine sound: a plane is flying low,
Time-efficient evolution rends the status quo.

Two old fogies hear a rumbling quake;
Looking out the window at the still-drained lake.
Suddenly a rushing sound, the dam has given way!
Wond'ring if they're going to make it to another day.
Watching as the water rises to the bottom step:
If this is the time to go, can they both accept?

Two old fogies gazing out to sea:
Noting the horizon, just past yonder tree.
List'nin' to the rumble of the engine of the ship.
Wishin' for at least *one* tumble on this trip!
Thinkin' of the first cruise when they never left the stateroom:
The start of all their children in that tiny Princess fate-room.

Two old fogies in a hurricane.
Each think the other is slightly less than sane.
Batten down the hatches, throw away the fear.
Secure all the latches, keep your courage near.
Thinking of each other, what's inside their head:
'How many layers will we have to shed?'

Two old fogies hobblin' down the lane,
Checkin' out the neighbors, searching every pane.
This one's left out all the trash, and that one's suckin' hash.
Rememberin' the night the cops came at the birthday bash.
Live a little, work a little, find some time to play,
"Yeah we had our time," they thought, "Oh that was sure the day!"

Two old fogies singin' in the pew.
The times they'd ever been to church had been so very few.
Looking at the sacristy, listening to the drone
Of the pretty preacher who knows not that she's alone.
What we could have taught her, given all of our years.
She would have had an explanation for her many tears.

Two old fogies huddle on a plane.
He says, "You forgot!" and she says "Not again!"
Going over every thing they might have brought, or not.
Lookin' out the window – all that's soon forgot.
Liftin' off to more adventure, "What is next?" the drive.
Cruisin' through the future, so to then feel more alive.

Two old fogies laying down to sleep.
Panties in a wee wad, covers in a heap;
Medicines all lined up, water in the cup,
Calculating hours 'til the next sunup.
Musing 'bout the next day, make priorities:
What other limits hail to these seniorities?

Two old fogies lying down to rest.
Insomnia meds are *surely* just a test.
Starin' at the ceiling, lookin' at the clock.
Did we bring the trash out? Did we check the lock?
Surface worries, like snow flurries, land and melt away.
Letting go to therefore grow - awake they meet the day.
Where is - - - S – L – E – E – E –E - P ?

Two old fogies lyin' in the sun.
One of 'em says, "Well, that sides' done!"
Checkin' out the brown spots and the white spots and the bumps,
Pokin' body here and there to check for any lumps.
Twenty years from d-day, or maybe it's tomorrow,
Look back over every day with pleasure mixed with sorrow.

Two old fogies shiver in the cold.
One hunches down, the other is bold.
Why accept restriction when there's always warmer climes?
Not much more to live now, they are runnin' outta times.
Zippin' up the jacket for the very last time,
Tradin' Boston Baked Beans for a very fresh lime.

Two old fogies sittin' by the pool:
One argues fate, the other argues rule
"'Twas God made this happen" said the one with the pipe.
"I want no such thing!" said the other at the hype.
Scoff met with pipe and decided to move over
There is, and there is not a thing called four-leaf-clover.

Two old fogies live another day.
Bert puts down his foot and lets the rocker sway.
Hangin' on the porch, the world in front a play.
The eyes are always open but the mind is oft away.
Bertie thinks of nothing and Gertie thinks of less
And that is why their house is such a great big mess!

Two old fogies push the grocery cart.
Gert adjusts her glasses while Bert attempts to fart.
Passin' by the meats and poultry there's a loud retort!
Everyone is acting like there's nothing to report.
Left to linger in the aisles, a scent of dark brown hue
Is all that's left of Gertie's try at cooking last night's stew.

Two old fogies restin' on a hill:
Sniffin' at the weiner dogs on someone else's grill.
Gertie's thinkin' birthdays, Bert is thinkin' steak,
Both remember good times at the cabin at the lake.
Bertie rises, wanders over, following his nose;
Gets invited, calls to Gertie, wakes her from a doze.

Two old fogies rowing in a boat.
Workin' really hard to keep it afloat.
Gert off the left, rowin' front to back;
Bert on the right, fingerin' his pocket snack.
Liftin' up the paddle seemed like such a giant chore.
Neither seemed to notice when the wind blew them to shore.

Two old fogies see Yosemite:
There for only hours – oh what a pity!
Nothing works at all in the old RV:
Water, electric, gas or satellite TV.
Hobbling down the mountain, to the RV shop,
Lost the fricken brakes halfway but pumped them to a stop.

Two old fogies settle down for sleep.
It's her birthday and Gert begins to weep.
"Now I'm old! I've just turned 65!"
Bert says, "Just be thankful you're alive!"
Looking old and feeling old are really not the issue
That is causing Gert to reach for tissue.

Two old fogies starin' at the screen
Both think the movie is one they've never seen.
The plot is familiar, the characters are new.
That it is a remake, they haven't got a clue.
"Same old, same old," grumbles testy Gert
"I ain't never seen it!" says an insistent Bert.

Two old fogies sittin' playin' Scrabble.
One tries to think while the other blathers babble.
There goes the 'x' on a triple word score.
There goes the 'q' which gets even more.
Listenin' to cicadas as the night falls low,
Trying to see the board in the porch light glow.

Two old fogies sunk on a soft couch:
One fallen forward, the other in a slouch.
Lost among the sliding shift of many memories.
Until poor Bert lets go a hootin' honkin' sneeze.
Gertie gives a gasp of fright as Bert pulls out his hankee
Gert pulls back her grasping hand from Bert's now inert wankee.

Two old fogies buzzin' 'round the mall:
Trying their damndest to experience it all.
Ice cream cone at one place, pizza at another,
Runnin' into folks who knew your best friend's brother.
Totin' bags and tummy's full, they head to find the car,
And then remember that the mall is sure not where they are.

Two old fogies climbin' down the stairs:
One is complaining, the other's splitting hairs.
Creaks in the staircase, creaks in the hips,
Slowly they descend, careful of the trips,
Thought flies by: "Stop the contention.
Feet, not brain, needs more of the attention."

Two old fogies, cryin' in their beer
"What'd we do wrong? How did we get here?"
"You said we'd have a house and you said we'd have a car.
Instead we're sitting starin' in the local bar."
"I did what I was told," said Bert about their life.
And Gertie said, "We didn't really count on all the strife."

Two old fogies floatin' in the pool.
One still hot, the other quite cool.
Conflict to a draw, each alone with their being;
Lookin' deeper in; but without: just not seein.'
Hand of hers bumps hand of his
And both see that *that* is all there is.

Two old fogies hear the telephone:
That clanging, banging instrument that says you're not alone.
Bertie knows that Gert will get it; Gert is in the loo,
Gertie shouts "HEL–LO!!" to Bert, she heard it ringing too.
Someone on the other end thinks they are not at home,
Leaving Gert and Bert to wonder why they're often alone.

Two old fogies finish up their soup;
The clatter of the spoons as the eyelids droop.
Full bellies churn as consciousness fades
One is switching lamps, the other's pulling shades.
Jeopardy and Fortune clang the winners on the set
Grizzled, knobby hands rest atop the family pet.

Two old fogies sittin' in a bar
One lived close and the other lived far.
Where will they live, and what will they do?
"Who will take care of me, will it be you?"
"It will be you," said the man with a smile.
"Who has it always been all this long while?"

Two old fogies sittin' in a kayak
One rowing forward, the other rowing back.
"Confound! This thing won't go!" says Bert
And sinks his paddle in the dirt.
Gert grabs his and hers as well
And dips them in the river's swell.

Two old fogies sittin' on the train:
Watchin' out the window at the pouring rain
Thinkin' of the hurricane that blew in '56
Takin' out the homestead with a whole life left to fix.
Three more home states would serve them apple pie,
None gave the answer to the question, "Why?"

Two old fogies typing up a storm.
Huddled in their afghans and tryin' to keep warm.
One is checking email, the other writes a book.
That's as long as neither leans a bit to take a look,
'Cause each one surreptitiously will often switch to games,
Thus avoiding verbal spats in which are hurled some names.

Two old fogies sittin' in their yard:
Watchin' all the relatives try so hard.
Babies, teens and middle life: one succeeds the other.
Flowin' oh-so-quickly by, oft without another.
Eat and poop and sleep and wake, it's right and wrong or black and white
Back and forth, and give and take: all is done with such poor sight.

Two old fogies watch the fireworks,
Wheelchair access to the front: one of the great perks.
Sparkles in the darkened sky, booms slightly delayed,
Thinking back to other Fourths when they both got paid.
Gertie sellin' hot dogs, Bert parked at the grill.
Never tiring of the party, watchin' with a thrill.

BERT DIES

Two old fogies starin' at the grate.
Both are unacquainted with the present time or date.
Musin' at the end of their long and brilliant run
Which had been frought with laughter, sadness, pain and fun.
"Pop" goes the ember as it fades from sight.
"Puff" goes his last breath, lookin' up to light.

GERTIE DIES

Gertie hears the pop and puff but doesn't lift her head.
Her heart and brain are quite aware that her old Bert is dead.
Thought is breath and breath is life;
Sadness thick as gravy, that splits with a knife;
Distance from the desolation, one last act of covering,
"O my God!" she thinks. "Is that an angel hovering?

Printed in the United States
by Baker & Taylor Publisher Services